LIGHT & CHEESY

50 Low Calorie Recipes for Cheese Lovers

Glenn Walton

Copyright © 2024 Glenn Walton

All rights reserved

No part of this book may be reproduced, or stored in a retrieval system, or transmitted in any form or by any means, electronic, mechanical, photocopying, recording, or otherwise, without express written permission of the publisher.

Cover design by: Buddy Jones

Printed in the United States of America

CONTENTS

Title Page
Copyright
Introduction   1
Cheese and Veggie Scramble   3
Cottage Cheese & Berry Bowl   6
Cheese & Spinach Egg Muffins   9
Ricotta and Peach Toast   12
Low Calorie Cheese Omelette   15
Cheesy Stuffed Mushrooms   18
Low Calorie Cheese Dip with Veggies   21
Cucumber and Cheese Bites   24
Greek Yogurt Cheese Spread on Whole Wheat Crackers   27
Light Caprese Salad with Fresh Mozzarella   30
Greek Salad with Feta Crumbles   33
Spinach Salad with Grated Parmesan   36
Cheesy Kale and Apple Salad   39
Open-Faced Turkey & Cheese Sandwich   42
Grilled Veggie & Cheese Wrap   45
Low Cal Cheese Quesadilla   48
Cheesy Cauliflower Soup   51
Mozzarella and Tomato Panini   54

Parmesan Crisps	57
Low Calorie Cheese Popcorn	60
String Cheese & Fruit Combo	62
Cheese-Stuffed Peppers	64
Cottage Cheese & Pineapple Snack	67
Baked Zucchini Boats with Cheese	69
Low Calorie Mac & Cheese	72
Cheesy Chicken & Broccoli Bake	75
Spinach and Ricotta-Stuffed Peppers	78
Cauliflower Crust Pizza with Cheese	81
Cheesy Cauliflower Mash	84
Parmesan Roasted Brussels Sprouts	87
Light Cheesy Mashed Potatoes	90
Cheesy Baked Asparagus	93
Grilled Corn with Cheese Topping	96
Ricotta Cheese & Honey Dessert	99
Low Calorie Cheesecake Bites	101
Cottage Cheese & Cinnamon Delight	104
Cheese-Stuffed Dates	106
Greek Yogurt & Cream Cheese Frosting with Berries	108
Cheese-Stuffed Mini Bell Peppers	111
Low-Calorie Cheese Nachos	114
Cheesy Zucchini Fritters	117
Cheese and Veggie Quiche Cups	120
Cottage Cheese & Cucumber Salad	123
Cheesy Baked Tomatoes	125
Cheese and Apple Slices	128
Cheesy Spinach Dip	130

Cheese-Stuffed Chicken Breast	133
Grilled Cheese Roll-Ups	136
Broccoli and Cheese Bites	139
Cheese and Avocado Toast	142
Nutritional Highlights	144
Cooking Tips	146
Serving Suggestions	148
Conclusion	150
We Appreciate Your Feedback!	151

INTRODUCTION

Cheese often gets a bad reputation in low-calorie diets, but the truth is, it can absolutely be part of a healthy eating plan without sacrificing flavor or enjoyment. Cheese is packed with protein, calcium, and essential nutrients that can help you feel fuller longer, making it a great addition to meals and snacks. The key is finding the right balance and making smart choices when it comes to the types of cheese you use and how much you incorporate into your diet. This book is all about helping you enjoy the cheesy flavors you love without the extra calories, proving that healthy eating doesn't have to mean giving up the foods you enjoy.

Brief Explanation Of How Cheese Can Be Enjoyed In A Low-Calorie Diet

Cheese can be part of a low-calorie diet if you focus on portion control and choose lighter options. Many types of cheese are lower in calories and fat than you might expect, such as mozzarella, cottage cheese, and feta. These varieties can be used in all kinds of meals, from salads to snacks, while still keeping your calorie intake in check. Additionally, pairing cheese with vegetables, fruits, or whole grains can help you feel satisfied with smaller amounts, allowing you to enjoy the cheesy goodness without overindulging. It's all about finding ways to incorporate cheese smartly and in moderation.

Tips For Choosing Low-Calorie Cheeses And

Portion Control

1. **Choose Naturally Lower-Calorie Cheeses:** Some cheeses are naturally lower in fat and calories. Soft cheeses like cottage cheese, ricotta, and part-skim mozzarella are great options that allow you to enjoy cheese while keeping calorie counts low. Goat cheese and feta are also flavorful, lower-calorie alternatives to richer cheeses like cheddar or brie.

2. **Look for Reduced-Fat Options:** Many popular cheeses, such as cheddar, Swiss, and provolone, are available in reduced-fat varieties. These versions have all the flavor you love but with fewer calories, making them a great choice for those looking to lighten up their meals.

3. **Focus on Portion Control:** Even lower-calorie cheeses can add up if you're not mindful of portions. A standard serving size of cheese is around one ounce, which is about the size of a pair of dice or a single slice from a block. Grating cheese or using small cubes instead of large slices can help you feel like you're eating more while sticking to appropriate portions.

4. **Pair Cheese with Low-Calorie Foods:** Cheese pairs beautifully with vegetables, fruits, and whole grains, all of which help you feel fuller while keeping your calorie intake in check. Combining cheese with high-volume, low-calorie ingredients allows you to enjoy cheesy flavors without overindulging. Think of salads topped with a sprinkle of feta, or a veggie omelette with a bit of grated mozzarella.

By making smart choices, you can enjoy all the rich, savory flavor of cheese while staying on track with your health and wellness goals. Let's dive into the recipes that will show you how!

CHEESE AND VEGGIE SCRAMBLE

Ingredients

- 2 large eggs (140 calories)
- ¼ cup shredded low-fat cheese (such as mozzarella or cheddar) (80 calories)
- ½ cup diced bell peppers (15 calories)
- ¼ cup diced onions (12 calories)
- ½ cup fresh spinach leaves (3 calories)
- 4 cherry tomatoes, halved (12 calories)
- 1 tablespoon olive oil (120 calories)
- Salt and pepper to taste (0 calories)

- Fresh parsley for garnish (optional, 0 calories)

Total Calories: Approximately 382 calories

Instructions

1. Heat the olive oil in a nonstick skillet over medium heat.
2. Add the bell peppers and onions to the skillet and sauté for 3-4 minutes until softened.
3. Add the spinach and cherry tomatoes to the skillet and cook for another 1-2 minutes until the spinach wilts.
4. In a bowl, whisk the eggs with a pinch of salt and pepper.
5. Pour the eggs into the skillet with the vegetables and scramble everything together for 2-3 minutes until the eggs are fully cooked.
6. Sprinkle the shredded cheese over the scramble and let it melt for 1 minute.
7. Serve hot, garnished with fresh parsley.

Tips And Tricks

- You can substitute other veggies like zucchini or mushrooms depending on what you have available.
- For extra protein, add in diced cooked chicken or turkey.

Tools Required

- Nonstick skillet
- Whisk

- Spatula

Fun Fact

Did you know that eggs are one of the best sources of complete protein? Pairing them with cheese and veggies makes for a well-rounded, satisfying breakfast!

Possible Ingredient Substitutions

- Swap regular cheese with plant-based cheese for a dairy-free option.
- Use egg whites instead of whole eggs to reduce the calorie content even further.

COTTAGE CHEESE & BERRY BOWL

Ingredients

- ½ cup low-fat cottage cheese (90 calories)
- ¼ cup strawberries, sliced (12 calories)
- ¼ cup blueberries (21 calories)
- ¼ cup raspberries (15 calories)
- 1 teaspoon honey (20 calories)
- 1 teaspoon chia seeds (20 calories)
- Fresh mint leaves for garnish (optional, 0 calories)

Total Calories: Approximately 178 calories

Instructions

1. In a bowl, add the cottage cheese as the base.
2. Top with sliced strawberries, blueberries, and raspberries.
3. Drizzle the honey over the berries for a touch of sweetness.
4. Sprinkle chia seeds on top for added texture and nutrients.
5. Garnish with fresh mint leaves if desired.

Tips And Tricks

- For extra crunch, you can add a few crushed nuts like almonds or walnuts, but keep in mind that it will increase the calorie count.
- If you prefer a sweeter dish, use a natural sweetener like stevia or agave syrup as a low-calorie alternative to honey.

Tools Required

- Mixing bowl
- Spoon for drizzling

Fun Fact

Cottage cheese is high in protein and low in fat, making it an excellent option for a quick, satisfying snack or breakfast that keeps you full longer!

Possible Ingredient Substitutions

- Use Greek yogurt instead of cottage cheese if you prefer a creamier texture.
- Swap out the berries for other fruits like sliced bananas or peaches.

CHEESE & SPINACH EGG MUFFINS

Ingredients

- 4 large eggs (280 calories)
- ½ cup shredded low-fat cheese (80 calories)
- 1 cup fresh spinach, chopped (7 calories)
- ¼ cup diced onions (12 calories)
- 1 tablespoon olive oil (120 calories)
- Salt and pepper to taste (0 calories)
- Fresh parsley for garnish (optional, 0 calories)

Total Calories: Approximately 499 calories (for 6 muffins, about 83 calories per muffin)

Instructions

1. Preheat the oven to 350°F (175°C) and grease a muffin tin with a bit of olive oil or cooking spray.
2. Heat the olive oil in a small pan over medium heat and sauté the onions until soft, about 3 minutes.
3. Add the chopped spinach and cook for an additional 2 minutes, until wilted. Remove from heat.
4. In a bowl, whisk together the eggs, shredded cheese, salt, and pepper.
5. Stir in the sautéed spinach and onions.
6. Divide the mixture evenly into the muffin tin, filling each section about ¾ full.
7. Bake for 15-20 minutes, or until the muffins are set and golden on top.
8. Let them cool for a few minutes before removing from the tin. Garnish with fresh parsley if desired.

Tips And Tricks

- These muffins can be stored in the fridge for up to 3 days, making them a great grab-and-go breakfast option.
- Feel free to add other veggies like diced bell peppers or mushrooms to switch up the flavor.

Tools Required

- Muffin tin
- Whisk

- Skillet for sautéing

Fun Fact

Egg muffins are an easy, protein-packed breakfast that you can customize with different ingredients to suit your taste!

Possible Ingredient Substitutions

- Use egg whites instead of whole eggs to cut down on calories.
- Swap regular cheese for plant-based cheese if you're going dairy-free.

RICOTTA AND PEACH TOAST

Ingredients

- 1 slice of whole grain bread (70 calories)
- ¼ cup ricotta cheese (60 calories)
- ½ fresh peach, sliced (30 calories)
- 1 teaspoon honey (20 calories)
- A pinch of cinnamon (0 calories)
- Fresh mint leaves for garnish (optional, 0 calories)

Total Calories: Approximately 180 calories

Instructions

1. Toast the slice of whole grain bread until golden brown.
2. Spread the ricotta cheese evenly over the toasted bread.
3. Arrange the peach slices on top of the ricotta.
4. Drizzle with honey and sprinkle a pinch of cinnamon for added flavor.
5. Garnish with fresh mint leaves for a refreshing finish.

Tips And Tricks

- You can swap peaches for other fruits like strawberries or figs depending on the season.
- For extra texture, add a sprinkle of crushed almonds or walnuts (but remember it will increase the calorie count).

Tools Required

- Toaster
- Knife for spreading

Fun Fact

Ricotta is an Italian cheese that's naturally low in fat compared to many other cheeses, making it a great choice for a lighter breakfast or snack!

Possible Ingredient Substitutions

- Use a low-fat or plant-based ricotta to reduce calories or make this dish vegan.

- Swap honey for agave syrup or maple syrup if you prefer a different sweetener.

LOW CALORIE CHEESE OMELETTE

Ingredients

- 2 large egg whites (34 calories)
- 1 large egg (70 calories)
- ¼ cup shredded low-fat cheese (80 calories)
- 1 tablespoon skim milk (5 calories)
- 1 teaspoon olive oil (40 calories)
- Salt and pepper to taste (0 calories)
- Fresh parsley for garnish (optional, 0 calories)
- Sliced tomatoes for serving (optional, 10 calories)

Total Calories: Approximately 239 calories

Instructions

1. In a bowl, whisk together the egg whites, whole egg, skim milk, salt, and pepper until smooth.
2. Heat the olive oil in a nonstick skillet over medium heat.
3. Pour the egg mixture into the skillet and cook for 2-3 minutes, or until the edges start to set.
4. Sprinkle the shredded cheese over half of the omelette, then fold the other half over the cheese.
5. Cook for another 1-2 minutes until the cheese melts and the omelette is fully cooked.
6. Serve hot, garnished with fresh parsley and sliced tomatoes on the side if desired.

Tips And Tricks

- For added veggies, you can sauté some spinach, mushrooms, or onions and fold them into the omelette.
- To make the omelette even lighter, use all egg whites instead of one whole egg.

Tools Required

- Nonstick skillet
- Whisk
- Spatula

Fun Fact

Eggs are one of the most versatile and nutrient-dense foods out there! They provide essential vitamins like B12 and vitamin D, making them an excellent choice for a healthy breakfast.

Possible Ingredient Substitutions

- Use a plant-based cheese if you're avoiding dairy.
- Swap the olive oil for a nonstick cooking spray to further reduce calories.

CHEESY STUFFED MUSHROOMS

Ingredients

- 12 medium button mushrooms (24 calories)
- ¼ cup low-fat cream cheese (80 calories)
- ¼ cup shredded low-fat mozzarella (80 calories)
- 1 tablespoon grated Parmesan cheese (22 calories)
- 1 clove garlic, minced (4 calories)
- 1 teaspoon olive oil (40 calories)
- Fresh parsley for garnish (optional, 0 calories)
- Salt and pepper to taste (0 calories)

Total Calories: Approximately 250 calories (for 12 mushrooms, about 21 calories per mushroom)

Instructions

1. Preheat your oven to 375°F (190°C).
2. Clean the mushrooms and remove the stems, creating a cavity for the filling.
3. In a small bowl, mix together the cream cheese, shredded mozzarella, grated Parmesan, garlic, olive oil, salt, and pepper.
4. Stuff each mushroom cap with the cheese mixture, filling them generously.
5. Place the mushrooms on a baking sheet and bake for 15-20 minutes, or until the cheese is melted and bubbly.
6. Garnish with fresh parsley before serving.

Tips And Tricks

- For added flavor, try adding chopped spinach or sun-dried tomatoes to the filling.
- If you're serving these at a party, prepare the filling ahead of time and stuff the mushrooms just before baking.

Tools Required

- Baking sheet
- Mixing bowl
- Spoon for stuffing

Fun Fact

Mushrooms are incredibly low in calories, making them the perfect vessel for a rich, cheesy filling that's still guilt-free!

Possible Ingredient Substitutions

- Use plant-based cheese for a dairy-free version.
- Swap button mushrooms for larger portobello mushrooms if you prefer a heartier appetizer.

LOW CALORIE CHEESE DIP WITH VEGGIES

Ingredients

- ½ cup low-fat cottage cheese (90 calories)
- ¼ cup Greek yogurt (30 calories)
- ¼ cup shredded low-fat cheddar cheese (80 calories)
- 1 tablespoon lemon juice (4 calories)
- 1 clove garlic, minced (4 calories)
- 1 tablespoon chopped fresh chives (0 calories)
- Salt and pepper to taste (0 calories)
- Assorted vegetables for dipping (carrots, cucumber, bell peppers, cherry tomatoes) (varies, approx. 50 calories for 1 cup)

Total Calories: Approximately 258 calories (including 1 cup of veggies for dipping)

Instructions

1. In a blender or food processor, combine the cottage cheese, Greek yogurt, shredded cheddar, lemon juice, garlic, salt, and pepper.
2. Blend until smooth and creamy.
3. Transfer the dip to a serving bowl and sprinkle chopped chives on top for garnish.
4. Serve with fresh, colorful vegetables such as carrots, cucumbers, bell peppers, and cherry tomatoes for dipping.

Tips And Tricks

- You can add a dash of hot sauce or smoked paprika to give the dip a little extra kick.
- To make it thicker, reduce the amount of Greek yogurt or add more shredded cheese.

Tools Required

- Blender or food processor
- Mixing bowl

Fun Fact

This dip is high in protein thanks to the cottage cheese and Greek yogurt, making it not only a delicious snack but also a filling one!

Possible Ingredient Substitutions

- Use a plant-based yogurt and cheese for a vegan version.
- Substitute any fresh herbs like parsley or dill for the chives based on your preference.

CUCUMBER AND CHEESE BITES

Ingredients

- 1 cucumber, sliced into rounds (30 calories)
- ¼ cup low-fat cream cheese (80 calories)
- ¼ cup shredded low-fat cheddar cheese (80 calories)
- 1 tablespoon fresh herbs (such as parsley or dill) for garnish (0 calories)
- Salt and pepper to taste (0 calories)

Total Calories: Approximately 190 calories (for 12-14 bites)

Instructions

1. Slice the cucumber into thin rounds and arrange them on a serving plate.
2. In a small bowl, mix the cream cheese with a pinch of salt and pepper.
3. Place a small dollop of cream cheese on each cucumber slice.
4. Sprinkle a bit of shredded cheddar cheese on top of the cream cheese.
5. Garnish with fresh herbs like parsley or dill for added flavor.
6. Serve chilled as a refreshing, low-calorie snack or appetizer.

Tips And Tricks

- You can add a slice of cherry tomato on top for extra color and flavor.
- For an extra kick, mix a bit of garlic powder or paprika into the cream cheese.

Tools Required

- Knife
- Small mixing bowl

Fun Fact

Cucumbers are over 95% water, making them a hydrating and low-calorie base for appetizers like this!

Possible Ingredient Substitutions

- Use a plant-based cream cheese and cheese for a vegan option.
- Swap the cucumber for zucchini slices if you prefer a different veggie base.

GREEK YOGURT CHEESE SPREAD ON WHOLE WHEAT CRACKERS

Ingredients

- ¼ cup Greek yogurt (30 calories)
- ¼ cup shredded low-fat mozzarella cheese (80 calories)
- 1 teaspoon lemon juice (4 calories)
- 1 teaspoon olive oil (40 calories)
- 8 whole wheat crackers (96 calories)
- Salt and pepper to taste (0 calories)
- Fresh herbs (such as parsley or dill) for garnish (0 calories)

Total Calories: Approximately 250 calories (for 8 crackers)

Instructions

1. In a small bowl, mix the Greek yogurt, shredded mozzarella, lemon juice, olive oil, salt, and pepper until smooth.
2. Spread the mixture evenly over each whole wheat cracker.
3. Garnish with fresh herbs like parsley or dill for added flavor.
4. Serve as a healthy snack or appetizer.

Tips And Tricks

- For extra flavor, add a pinch of garlic powder or chili flakes to the yogurt mixture.
- These are great to serve at a party or as a quick snack.

Tools Required

- Mixing bowl
- Spoon for spreading

Fun Fact

Greek yogurt is an excellent source of protein and pairs well with cheese for a creamy, satisfying spread that feels indulgent without being too high in calories.

Possible Ingredient Substitutions

- Use whole grain or gluten-free crackers if you prefer.
- Swap the mozzarella for a stronger-flavored cheese like sharp cheddar for an extra kick.

LIGHT CAPRESE SALAD WITH FRESH MOZZARELLA

Ingredients

- 1 large ripe tomato, sliced (30 calories)
- 2 ounces fresh mozzarella, sliced (140 calories)
- 6 fresh basil leaves (0 calories)
- 1 teaspoon balsamic vinegar (5 calories)
- 1 teaspoon olive oil (40 calories)
- Salt and pepper to taste (0 calories)

Total Calories: Approximately 215 calories

Instructions

1. Arrange alternating slices of tomato and fresh mozzarella on a serving plate.
2. Tuck fresh basil leaves between the slices of tomato and mozzarella.
3. Drizzle with olive oil and balsamic vinegar.
4. Season with salt and pepper to taste.
5. Serve immediately as a light and refreshing appetizer or side dish.

Tips And Tricks

- For a lower-calorie version, use less mozzarella or opt for a light mozzarella.
- You can add a sprinkle of crushed red pepper for a bit of heat.

Tools Required

- Knife for slicing
- Serving plate

Fun Fact

Caprese salad is named after the island of Capri in Italy, where it's believed the dish originated! The colors of the salad represent the Italian flag.

Possible Ingredient Substitutions

- Use a balsamic glaze instead of vinegar for a slightly sweeter taste.
- Add avocado slices for extra creaminess, though it will add a few more calories.

GREEK SALAD WITH FETA CRUMBLES

Ingredients

- 1 cup chopped cucumber (16 calories)
- 1 cup chopped tomatoes (30 calories)
- ¼ cup sliced red onion (12 calories)
- ¼ cup black olives (50 calories)
- 2 tablespoons crumbled feta cheese (50 calories)
- 1 tablespoon olive oil (120 calories)
- 1 tablespoon lemon juice (4 calories)
- Fresh oregano leaves for garnish (optional, 0 calories)
- Salt and pepper to taste (0 calories)

Total Calories: Approximately 282 calories

Instructions

1. In a large bowl, combine the cucumber, tomatoes, red onion, and black olives.
2. Drizzle with olive oil and lemon juice. Toss gently to combine.
3. Sprinkle crumbled feta cheese over the top.
4. Garnish with fresh oregano leaves and season with salt and pepper to taste.
5. Serve chilled as a refreshing, light salad.

Tips And Tricks

- You can add chopped green bell peppers for more crunch and flavor.
- For a lighter version, use less olive oil or replace with a balsamic vinaigrette.

Tools Required

- Mixing bowl
- Knife for chopping

Fun Fact

Feta cheese is a staple in Greek cuisine and is made from sheep's milk or a mixture of sheep and goat milk. Its tangy, rich flavor complements the freshness of vegetables perfectly!

Possible Ingredient Substitutions

- Use Kalamata olives for a more authentic Greek flavor.
- Swap out feta for goat cheese if you prefer a milder taste.

SPINACH SALAD WITH GRATED PARMESAN

Ingredients

- 2 cups fresh spinach leaves (14 calories)
- ¼ cup grated Parmesan cheese (108 calories)
- ¼ cup thinly sliced red onions (12 calories)
- ½ cup cherry tomatoes, halved (15 calories)
- 1 tablespoon olive oil (120 calories)
- 1 tablespoon lemon juice (4 calories)
- Freshly ground black pepper to taste (0 calories)

Total Calories: Approximately 273 calories

Instructions

1. In a large bowl, combine the fresh spinach leaves, red onions, and halved cherry tomatoes.
2. Drizzle with olive oil and lemon juice. Toss gently to coat the spinach.
3. Sprinkle the grated Parmesan cheese over the salad.
4. Season with freshly ground black pepper to taste.
5. Serve immediately as a light and refreshing salad.

Tips And Tricks

- For extra flavor, you can toast the Parmesan cheese in the oven for a crispy topping.
- Add a hard-boiled egg for extra protein, but keep in mind it will increase the calorie count.

Tools Required

- Mixing bowl
- Knife for slicing

Fun Fact

Spinach is packed with iron, vitamins, and antioxidants, making it one of the healthiest leafy greens! Pairing it with Parmesan adds a savory touch that enhances its flavor.

Possible Ingredient Substitutions

- Use arugula instead of spinach for a more peppery

flavor.

- Swap Parmesan for a plant-based alternative if you want a dairy-free option.

CHEESY KALE AND APPLE SALAD

Ingredients

- 2 cups chopped kale (33 calories)
- ½ medium apple, thinly sliced (45 calories)
- ¼ cup crumbled low-fat cheese (such as feta or goat cheese) (80 calories)
- 1 tablespoon olive oil (120 calories)
- 1 tablespoon lemon juice (4 calories)
- 1 tablespoon chopped walnuts or almonds (45 calories)
- Salt and pepper to taste (0 calories)

Total Calories: Approximately 327 calories

Instructions

1. In a large bowl, massage the chopped kale with olive oil and lemon juice for 1-2 minutes to soften the leaves.
2. Add the thinly sliced apples and crumbled cheese to the kale.
3. Sprinkle the chopped nuts over the salad.
4. Season with salt and pepper to taste.
5. Toss everything gently to combine and serve fresh.

Tips And Tricks

- Massaging the kale with olive oil helps break down its fibrous texture, making it more tender and easier to eat.
- You can add dried cranberries or raisins for a bit of sweetness, but keep in mind this will add to the calorie count.

Tools Required

- Mixing bowl
- Knife for slicing

Fun Fact

Kale is a nutrient-dense superfood, packed with vitamins A, C, and K, as well as calcium, making it a great base for this hearty salad.

Possible Ingredient Substitutions

- Use spinach or arugula instead of kale if you prefer a milder green.
- Swap the cheese for a dairy-free alternative for a vegan version of this salad.

OPEN-FACED TURKEY & CHEESE SANDWICH

Ingredients

- 1 slice of whole wheat bread (70 calories)
- 2 ounces of sliced turkey breast (60 calories)
- ¼ cup shredded low-fat cheddar cheese (80 calories)
- 1 tablespoon Dijon mustard (10 calories)
- A few leaves of fresh spinach or arugula (5 calories)
- Salt and pepper to taste (0 calories)

Total Calories: Approximately 225 calories

Instructions

LIGHT & CHEESY

1. Preheat the oven to 350°F (175°C).
2. Spread the Dijon mustard over the slice of whole wheat bread.
3. Layer the sliced turkey breast on top of the bread.
4. Sprinkle the shredded cheese evenly over the turkey.
5. Place the sandwich on a baking sheet and bake for 5-7 minutes, or until the cheese is melted and bubbly.
6. Remove from the oven and top with fresh spinach or arugula leaves.
7. Season with salt and pepper to taste, and serve immediately.

Tips And Tricks

- For added flavor, you can toast the bread slightly before assembling the sandwich.
- If you prefer a cold sandwich, simply skip the baking step and enjoy it as is.

Tools Required

- Baking sheet
- Knife for spreading

Fun Fact

Open-faced sandwiches are a great way to enjoy a hearty meal while cutting back on calories from extra bread!

Possible Ingredient Substitutions

- Use a different type of cheese, like Swiss or provolone, for a variation in flavor.
- Substitute turkey with chicken slices if preferred.

GRILLED VEGGIE & CHEESE WRAP

Ingredients

- 1 whole wheat tortilla (100 calories)
- ½ cup grilled mixed vegetables (bell peppers, zucchini, onions) (40 calories)
- ¼ cup shredded low-fat mozzarella cheese (80 calories)
- 1 tablespoon olive oil (120 calories)
- Salt and pepper to taste (0 calories)

Total Calories: Approximately 340 calories

Instructions

1. Heat the olive oil in a grill pan over medium heat.
2. Add the sliced bell peppers, zucchini, and onions to the pan and grill for about 5-7 minutes, until tender and slightly charred.
3. Remove the veggies from the pan and set aside.
4. Lay the whole wheat tortilla flat and sprinkle the shredded cheese down the center.
5. Add the grilled vegetables on top of the cheese.
6. Fold the sides of the tortilla over the filling and roll it up tightly.
7. Return the wrap to the grill pan and cook for 1-2 minutes on each side, until the cheese is melted and the tortilla is lightly toasted.
8. Slice the wrap in half and serve immediately.

Tips And Tricks

- You can add a dollop of hummus or pesto inside the wrap for extra flavor.
- For a lighter option, reduce the amount of cheese or skip the olive oil and use a nonstick spray instead.

Tools Required

- Grill pan or skillet
- Tongs for grilling

Fun Fact

Grilled veggie wraps are a great way to pack in a variety of colorful vegetables, making them not only delicious but also nutrient-dense!

Possible Ingredient Substitutions

- Use a low-carb tortilla to reduce the calorie count further.
- Add spinach or kale for more greens and crunch.

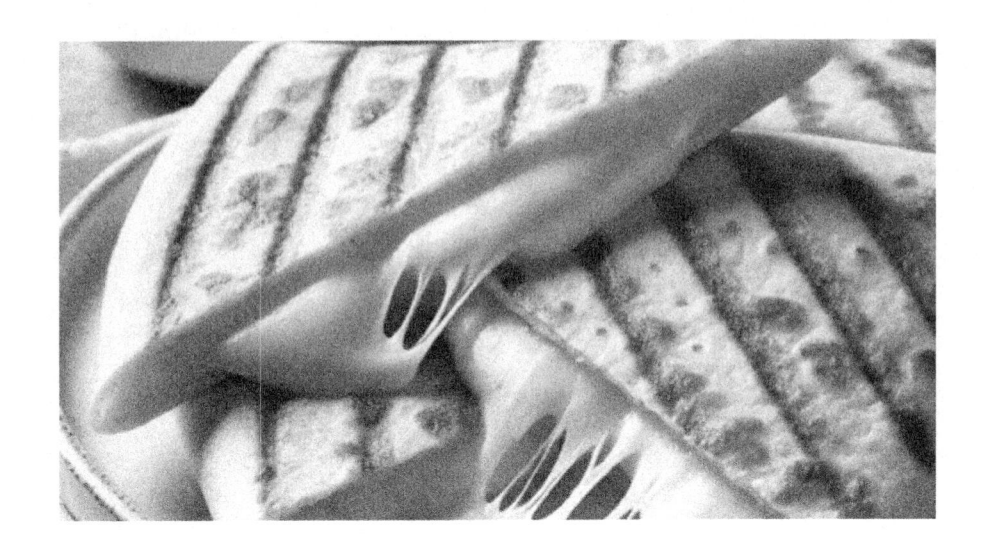

LOW CAL CHEESE QUESADILLA

Ingredients

- 1 whole wheat tortilla (100 calories)
- ¼ cup shredded low-fat cheddar cheese (80 calories)
- 1 teaspoon olive oil or nonstick spray (40 calories)
- Salsa for dipping (optional, 10 calories per tablespoon)
- Fresh herbs for garnish (optional, 0 calories)

Total Calories: Approximately 220 calories

Instructions

1. Heat a nonstick skillet over medium heat and add a

teaspoon of olive oil or use nonstick spray.

2. Place the whole wheat tortilla in the skillet and sprinkle the shredded cheese evenly on one half of the tortilla.
3. Fold the tortilla over to create a half-moon shape and cook for 2-3 minutes on each side, until the cheese is melted and the tortilla is golden brown.
4. Remove the quesadilla from the skillet and let it cool for a minute before cutting it into triangles.
5. Serve with a side of salsa and garnish with fresh herbs if desired.

Tips And Tricks

- For extra flavor, you can add some grilled veggies or a sprinkle of seasoning like cumin or chili powder inside the quesadilla.
- Serve with guacamole or Greek yogurt for a healthy dipping option.

Tools Required

- Nonstick skillet
- Spatula

Fun Fact

Quesadillas are a Mexican classic and can be easily modified to fit a low-calorie diet by using whole wheat tortillas and low-fat cheese!

Possible Ingredient Substitutions

- Use a low-carb or gluten-free tortilla if needed.
- Substitute cheddar with a plant-based cheese for a dairy-free option.

CHEESY CAULIFLOWER SOUP

Ingredients

- 3 cups cauliflower florets (75 calories)
- 1 cup low-sodium vegetable broth (10 calories)
- 1 cup skim milk (80 calories)
- ½ cup shredded low-fat cheddar cheese (160 calories)
- 1 clove garlic, minced (4 calories)
- 1 tablespoon olive oil (120 calories)
- Salt and pepper to taste (0 calories)
- Fresh parsley for garnish (optional, 0 calories)

Total Calories: Approximately 449 calories (serves 2, about 225 calories per serving)

Instructions

1. Heat the olive oil in a large pot over medium heat. Add the minced garlic and sauté for 1-2 minutes until fragrant.
2. Add the cauliflower florets and vegetable broth to the pot. Bring to a boil, then reduce heat and simmer for 10-12 minutes until the cauliflower is tender.
3. Using an immersion blender, blend the cauliflower mixture until smooth and creamy.
4. Stir in the skim milk and shredded cheese, cooking over low heat until the cheese is fully melted and the soup is thickened.
5. Season with salt and pepper to taste.
6. Serve hot, garnished with fresh parsley and an extra sprinkle of cheese if desired.

Tips And Tricks

- You can add a pinch of nutmeg for a subtle flavor boost.
- If you prefer a thicker soup, reduce the amount of vegetable broth or add more cauliflower.

Tools Required

- Large pot
- Immersion blender (or regular blender)

Fun Fact

Cauliflower is an excellent low-calorie vegetable that's rich in fiber and antioxidants, making it a great base for creamy soups like this one!

Possible Ingredient Substitutions

- Use almond milk instead of skim milk for a dairy-free version.
- Add a pinch of smoked paprika for a slightly smoky flavor.

MOZZARELLA AND TOMATO PANINI

Ingredients

- 2 slices whole grain bread (140 calories)
- 2 ounces fresh mozzarella cheese (140 calories)
- 1 medium tomato, sliced (22 calories)
- 1 teaspoon olive oil (40 calories)
- Salt and pepper to taste (0 calories)
- Fresh basil leaves (optional, 0 calories)

Total Calories: Approximately 342 calories

Instructions

1. Preheat a panini press or grill pan over medium heat.
2. Brush the outer sides of the whole grain bread slices with olive oil.
3. Place fresh mozzarella slices and tomato slices on one side of the bread.
4. Add fresh basil leaves (optional), and season with salt and pepper.
5. Close the sandwich with the other slice of bread and place it in the panini press.
6. Grill for 3-5 minutes, or until the bread is golden and crispy, and the cheese is melted.
7. Remove from the grill, cut in half, and serve hot.

Tips And Tricks

- For an extra flavor boost, drizzle a little balsamic glaze over the tomatoes before grilling.
- If you don't have a panini press, you can use a regular skillet and press the sandwich down with a spatula.

Tools Required

- Panini press or grill pan
- Spatula

Fun Fact

The combination of mozzarella, tomato, and basil is a classic Italian pairing known as "Caprese," which is popular in salads, sandwiches, and pizzas.

Possible Ingredient Substitutions

- Use a low-carb or gluten-free bread if preferred.
- Substitute mozzarella with a dairy-free cheese for a vegan option.

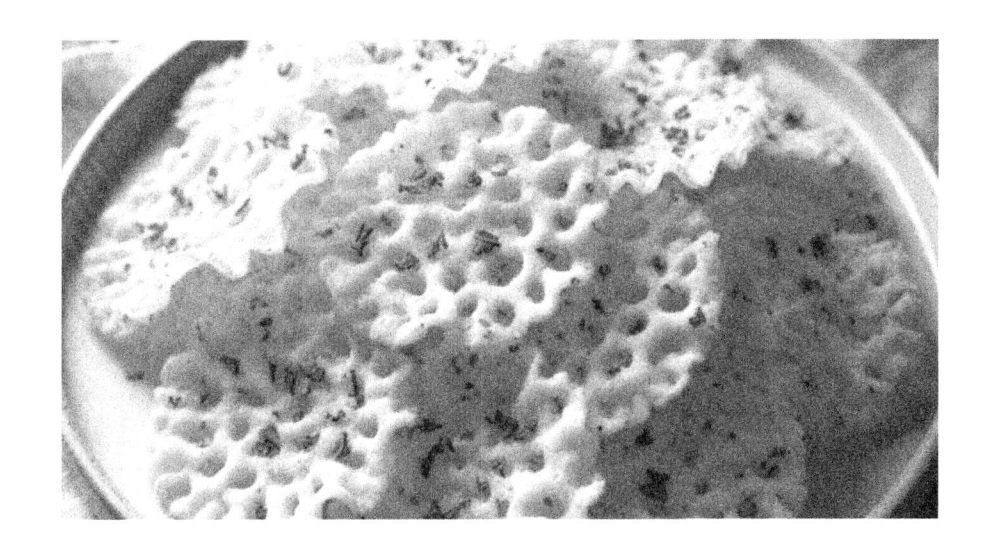

PARMESAN CRISPS

Ingredients

- 1 cup grated Parmesan cheese (431 calories)
- Fresh herbs like parsley for garnish (optional, 0 calories)
- Black pepper or red pepper flakes for seasoning (optional, 0 calories)

Total Calories: Approximately 431 calories (makes 12-15 crisps, about 29-36 calories per crisp)

Instructions

1. Preheat your oven to 400°F (200°C) and line a baking sheet with parchment paper.
2. Scoop 1 tablespoon of grated Parmesan cheese onto the

parchment paper, creating small mounds. Space them out evenly.

3. Flatten each mound slightly with the back of a spoon to create thin circles.
4. Optional: Sprinkle black pepper or red pepper flakes over the cheese for added flavor.
5. Bake for 5-7 minutes, or until the crisps are golden and bubbly.
6. Remove from the oven and let the crisps cool on the baking sheet for a few minutes before transferring them to a plate.
7. Garnish with fresh parsley or other herbs if desired, and serve.

Tips And Tricks

- Parmesan crisps can be stored in an airtight container for up to 3 days, making them a great snack to prepare ahead of time.
- These crisps are perfect for adding a crunchy element to salads or soups.

Tools Required

- Baking sheet
- Parchment paper
- Spatula

Fun Fact

Parmesan crisps are naturally gluten-free and low-carb, making them a popular snack for those following keto or low-carb diets.

Possible Ingredient Substitutions

- Try using other hard cheeses like Asiago or Pecorino Romano for a different flavor.
- Add a sprinkle of garlic powder or Italian seasoning for an extra flavor boost.

LOW CALORIE CHEESE POPCORN

Ingredients

- 3 cups air-popped popcorn (93 calories)
- 1 tablespoon grated Parmesan cheese (22 calories)
- 1 teaspoon cheese powder (like cheddar cheese seasoning) (15 calories)
- 1 teaspoon olive oil or butter spray (40 calories)
- Salt to taste (0 calories)

Total Calories: Approximately 170 calories

Instructions

1. In a large bowl, toss the air-popped popcorn with olive oil or butter spray to lightly coat it.
2. Sprinkle the grated Parmesan cheese and cheese powder over the popcorn, tossing to evenly distribute.
3. Season with a pinch of salt to taste.
4. Serve immediately as a light, cheesy snack.

Tips And Tricks

- You can adjust the cheese seasoning to your preference, adding more or less depending on how cheesy you want it.
- For a spicy twist, add a dash of paprika or chili powder to the popcorn.

Tools Required

- Large mixing bowl
- Air popper (or stove for popping popcorn)

Fun Fact

Popcorn is a whole grain that's naturally low in calories, making it a great base for light, savory snacks like this cheesy version!

Possible Ingredient Substitutions

- Use nutritional yeast as a cheesy, dairy-free alternative to Parmesan.
- Swap the olive oil for a nonstick spray if you want to reduce the calorie count even further.

STRING CHEESE & FRUIT COMBO

Ingredients

- 1 piece of low-fat string cheese (70 calories)
- ½ apple, sliced (45 calories)
- ½ cup grapes (31 calories)
- 3 medium strawberries (12 calories)

Total Calories: Approximately 158 calories

Instructions

1. Arrange the string cheese on a plate alongside the sliced apples, grapes, and strawberries.
2. Serve as a simple, nutritious snack that's both

satisfying and balanced.

Tips And Tricks

- You can substitute the fruits based on what's in season, such as blueberries or oranges.
- If you're looking for extra crunch, pair the fruit with a small handful of almonds or walnuts (but remember to adjust the calorie count).

Tools Required

- Knife for slicing the fruit
- Serving plate

Fun Fact

String cheese is a great portable snack that's rich in protein, and pairing it with fruit adds fiber and natural sweetness to your snack.

Possible Ingredient Substitutions

- Use a plant-based string cheese for a dairy-free option.
- Swap apples for pears or peaches for a different flavor profile.

CHEESE-STUFFED PEPPERS

Ingredients

- 6 mini bell peppers, halved and seeded (36 calories)
- ¼ cup low-fat cream cheese (80 calories)
- ¼ cup shredded low-fat cheddar cheese (80 calories)
- 1 clove garlic, minced (4 calories)
- 1 teaspoon olive oil (40 calories)
- Fresh herbs for garnish (optional, 0 calories)
- Salt and pepper to taste (0 calories)

Total Calories: Approximately 240 calories

Instructions

1. Preheat the oven to 375°F (190°C).
2. In a small bowl, mix the cream cheese, shredded cheddar cheese, garlic, salt, and pepper.
3. Stuff each halved mini pepper with the cheese mixture.
4. Drizzle the peppers with olive oil and place them on a baking sheet.
5. Bake for 15-20 minutes, or until the cheese is melted and golden brown on top.
6. Garnish with fresh herbs and serve hot.

Tips And Tricks

- You can add a sprinkle of breadcrumbs on top for extra crunch, but keep in mind it will add more calories.
- Serve these as appetizers or side dishes at parties, as they're easy to make and a crowd-pleaser.

Tools Required

- Baking sheet
- Small mixing bowl
- Knife for halving the peppers

Fun Fact

Mini bell peppers are naturally sweet and full of vitamins A and C, making them a nutritious base for this cheesy filling.

Possible Ingredient Substitutions

- Use goat cheese or ricotta in place of cream cheese for a different flavor.
- Add chopped spinach or sun-dried tomatoes to the cheese mixture for added texture and taste.

COTTAGE CHEESE & PINEAPPLE SNACK

Ingredients

- ½ cup low-fat cottage cheese (90 calories)
- ½ cup fresh pineapple chunks (40 calories)
- 1 teaspoon chia seeds (20 calories)
- Fresh mint for garnish (optional, 0 calories)

Total Calories: Approximately 150 calories

Instructions

1. In a small bowl, add the cottage cheese as the base.
2. Top with fresh pineapple chunks and sprinkle chia seeds over the top.

3. Garnish with fresh mint for an extra touch of flavor if desired.
4. Serve chilled as a refreshing and protein-packed snack.

Tips And Tricks

- You can swap out the pineapple for other fruits like mango, peach, or berries if you prefer.
- Add a drizzle of honey for extra sweetness, but keep in mind that it will increase the calorie count.

Tools Required

- Small bowl

Fun Fact

Cottage cheese is high in protein, making it a great option for a snack that keeps you full longer. Pairing it with pineapple adds natural sweetness and tropical flavor!

Possible Ingredient Substitutions

- Use Greek yogurt instead of cottage cheese if you prefer a creamier texture.
- For a lower-calorie option, skip the chia seeds or use less.

BAKED ZUCCHINI BOATS WITH CHEESE

Ingredients

- 2 medium zucchinis, halved lengthwise and hollowed out (66 calories)
- ½ cup shredded low-fat mozzarella cheese (160 calories)
- ¼ cup grated Parmesan cheese (110 calories)
- 1 clove garlic, minced (4 calories)
- 1 tablespoon olive oil (120 calories)
- Fresh herbs for garnish (optional, 0 calories)
- Salt and pepper to taste (0 calories)

Total Calories: Approximately 460 calories (for 4 boats)

Instructions

1. Preheat the oven to 375°F (190°C).
2. Brush the hollowed-out zucchini halves with olive oil and season with salt and pepper.
3. In a small bowl, mix the shredded mozzarella, Parmesan, and minced garlic.
4. Fill each zucchini half with the cheese mixture.
5. Place the stuffed zucchinis on a baking sheet and bake for 15-20 minutes, or until the cheese is melted and golden brown, and the zucchini is tender.
6. Garnish with fresh herbs and serve hot.

Tips And Tricks

- You can add cooked quinoa or ground turkey to the filling for extra protein.
- Try sprinkling some red pepper flakes on top for a bit of heat.

Tools Required

- Baking sheet
- Knife for hollowing zucchinis
- Small mixing bowl

Fun Fact

Zucchini is a versatile vegetable that's low in calories and high in vitamins, making it an excellent choice for light and healthy meals!

Possible Ingredient Substitutions

- Use vegan cheese to make this dish dairy-free.
- Swap zucchini for yellow squash if you prefer a different flavor.

LOW CALORIE MAC & CHEESE

Ingredients

- 1 cup cooked whole wheat macaroni (180 calories)
- ½ cup shredded low-fat cheddar cheese (160 calories)
- ¼ cup skim milk (22 calories)
- 1 tablespoon light cream cheese (30 calories)
- 1 teaspoon olive oil (40 calories)
- Salt and pepper to taste (0 calories)
- A pinch of paprika or garlic powder (optional, 0 calories)

Total Calories: Approximately 432 calories (serves 2, about 216 calories per serving)

Instructions

1. In a saucepan, heat the olive oil over medium heat. Add the skim milk and light cream cheese, stirring until smooth and heated through.
2. Gradually add the shredded cheddar cheese, stirring constantly until melted and fully incorporated into a creamy sauce.
3. Season with salt, pepper, and optional paprika or garlic powder.
4. Toss the cooked macaroni in the cheese sauce until well coated.
5. Serve hot, garnished with a sprinkle of extra cheese if desired.

Tips And Tricks

- You can use cauliflower in place of some of the macaroni for a lower-calorie option.
- Adding a pinch of mustard powder to the sauce can enhance the cheesy flavor.

Tools Required

- Saucepan
- Spoon for stirring

Fun Fact

Mac & Cheese is one of the ultimate comfort foods, but you can still enjoy it guilt-free by using lower-calorie ingredients like light cheese and whole wheat pasta!

Possible Ingredient Substitutions

- Use plant-based cheese and almond milk for a vegan version.
- Substitute regular pasta for chickpea or lentil pasta to boost the protein content.

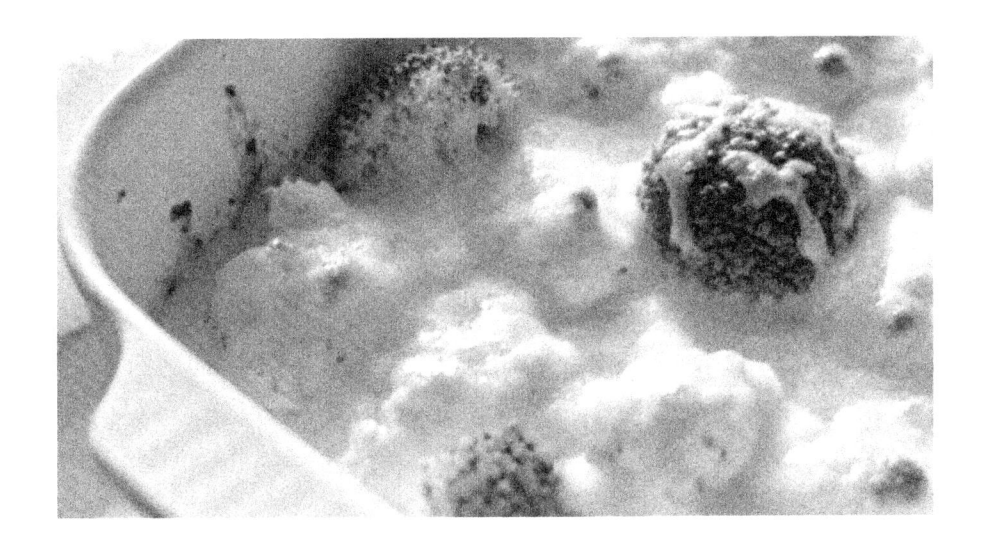

CHEESY CHICKEN & BROCCOLI BAKE

Ingredients

- 1 cup cooked chicken breast, diced (165 calories)
- 2 cups broccoli florets, steamed (62 calories)
- ½ cup shredded low-fat cheddar cheese (160 calories)
- ¼ cup light cream cheese (60 calories)
- ¼ cup skim milk (22 calories)
- 1 clove garlic, minced (4 calories)
- 1 tablespoon olive oil (120 calories)
- Salt and pepper to taste (0 calories)

Total Calories: Approximately 593 calories (serves 2, about 297 calories per serving)

Instructions

1. Preheat the oven to 375°F (190°C).
2. In a large skillet, heat the olive oil over medium heat and sauté the garlic for 1-2 minutes until fragrant.
3. Add the steamed broccoli and diced chicken breast to the skillet and stir to combine.
4. In a separate bowl, whisk together the light cream cheese, skim milk, and half of the shredded cheddar cheese until smooth.
5. Pour the cheese mixture over the chicken and broccoli, stirring to coat evenly.
6. Transfer the mixture to a casserole dish and top with the remaining cheddar cheese.
7. Bake for 15-20 minutes, or until the cheese is melted and bubbly.
8. Serve hot.

Tips And Tricks

- You can add a sprinkle of breadcrumbs on top before baking for a crunchy texture, though it will add a few more calories.
- For extra flavor, mix in some herbs like thyme or rosemary.

Tools Required

- Skillet
- Casserole dish

Fun Fact

Broccoli is rich in vitamins and fiber, making it the perfect companion to lean chicken in this comforting, cheesy bake.

Possible Ingredient Substitutions

- Use turkey instead of chicken if you prefer.
- For a low-carb option, replace the milk with almond or coconut milk.

SPINACH AND RICOTTA-STUFFED PEPPERS

Ingredients

- 4 medium bell peppers, halved and seeded (96 calories)
- 1 cup ricotta cheese (240 calories)
- 1 cup fresh spinach, chopped (7 calories)
- ¼ cup grated Parmesan cheese (110 calories)
- 1 clove garlic, minced (4 calories)
- 1 tablespoon olive oil (120 calories)
- Salt and pepper to taste (0 calories)
- Fresh herbs for garnish (optional, 0 calories)

Total Calories: Approximately 577 calories (serves 4, about 144 calories per serving)

Instructions

1. Preheat the oven to 375°F (190°C).
2. In a skillet, heat the olive oil over medium heat and sauté the garlic and chopped spinach until the spinach wilts.
3. In a bowl, mix the ricotta cheese, sautéed spinach, salt, and pepper.
4. Stuff each halved bell pepper with the spinach and ricotta mixture.
5. Place the stuffed peppers on a baking sheet and sprinkle with grated Parmesan.
6. Bake for 20-25 minutes, or until the peppers are tender and the cheese is golden and bubbly.
7. Garnish with fresh herbs and serve hot.

Tips And Tricks

- You can add a pinch of red pepper flakes to the filling for some heat.
- This dish can be prepared ahead of time and baked just before serving.

Tools Required

- Baking sheet
- Skillet for sautéing

Fun Fact

Bell peppers are a great source of vitamin C and antioxidants, making this dish both nutritious and delicious!

Possible Ingredient Substitutions

- Use cottage cheese instead of ricotta for a lower-calorie version.
- Substitute spinach with kale or arugula for a different green.

CAULIFLOWER CRUST PIZZA WITH CHEESE

Ingredients

- 1 small head of cauliflower, grated (150 calories)
- ½ cup shredded low-fat mozzarella cheese (160 calories)
- ¼ cup grated Parmesan cheese (110 calories)
- 1 large egg, beaten (70 calories)
- 1 teaspoon Italian seasoning (0 calories)
- Salt and pepper to taste (0 calories)
- Fresh basil leaves for garnish (optional, 0 calories)

Total Calories: Approximately 490 calories (serves 2, about 245 calories per serving)

Instructions

1. Preheat the oven to 400°F (200°C) and line a baking sheet with parchment paper.
2. Grate the cauliflower and steam it for 5 minutes until softened. Let it cool, then press out the excess moisture using a clean kitchen towel or paper towel.
3. In a bowl, combine the grated cauliflower, beaten egg, shredded mozzarella, Parmesan, Italian seasoning, salt, and pepper. Mix well.
4. Press the cauliflower mixture into a round pizza shape on the prepared baking sheet.
5. Bake the crust for 15-20 minutes, or until golden and firm.
6. Remove the crust from the oven and top with additional mozzarella cheese.
7. Bake for another 5-7 minutes, or until the cheese is melted and bubbly.
8. Garnish with fresh basil leaves and serve hot.

Tips And Tricks

- For added flavor, you can sprinkle garlic powder or red pepper flakes on top of the cheese before baking.
- This crust works well with any of your favorite pizza toppings, such as veggies, chicken, or fresh herbs.

Tools Required

- Baking sheet
- Grater

- Kitchen towel or paper towel for pressing the cauliflower

Fun Fact

Cauliflower is a great low-carb substitute for traditional pizza crusts, making this recipe both healthy and satisfying!

Possible Ingredient Substitutions

- Use almond flour or a store-bought cauliflower pizza crust if you prefer.
- Add a plant-based cheese for a dairy-free version.

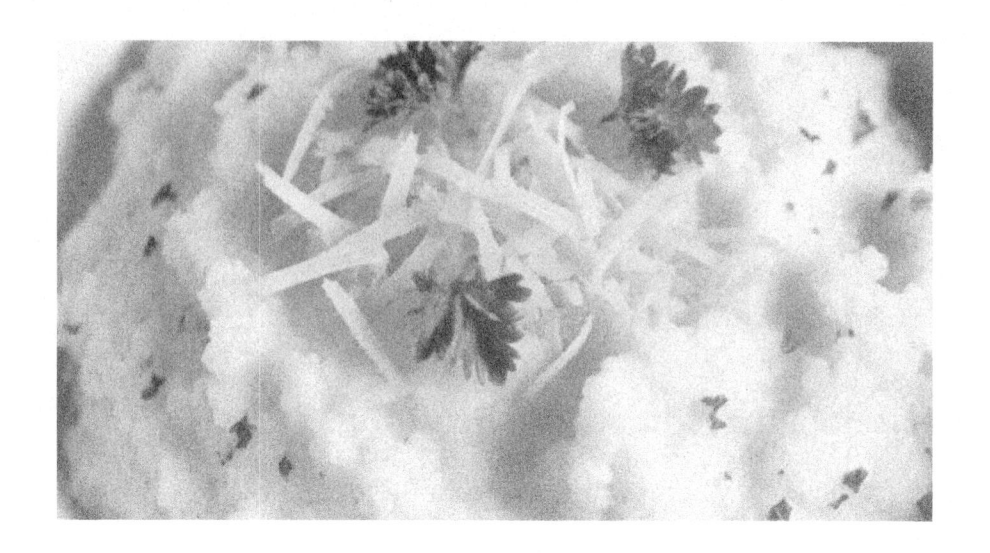

CHEESY CAULIFLOWER MASH

Ingredients

- 1 medium head of cauliflower, cut into florets (150 calories)
- ½ cup shredded low-fat cheddar cheese (160 calories)
- ¼ cup skim milk (22 calories)
- 1 tablespoon light cream cheese (30 calories)
- 1 tablespoon olive oil (120 calories)
- Salt and pepper to taste (0 calories)
- Fresh parsley for garnish (optional, 0 calories)

Total Calories: Approximately 482 calories (serves 4, about 120 calories per serving)

Instructions

1. Steam the cauliflower florets for 10-12 minutes until tender.
2. Drain the cauliflower and transfer it to a blender or food processor.
3. Add the shredded cheddar cheese, cream cheese, olive oil, and skim milk. Blend until smooth and creamy.
4. Season with salt and pepper to taste.
5. Transfer the mash to a serving bowl and garnish with fresh parsley and an extra sprinkle of cheese if desired.

Tips And Tricks

- For a smoother consistency, blend the cauliflower longer or add a bit more milk.
- You can add a pinch of garlic powder or paprika for extra flavor.

Tools Required

- Blender or food processor
- Steamer or pot for steaming the cauliflower

Fun Fact

Cauliflower is a great low-carb substitute for potatoes, making this cheesy mash a lighter, healthier option that's still satisfying!

Possible Ingredient Substitutions

- Use almond milk for a dairy-free version.
- Add a bit of Parmesan cheese for extra savory flavor.

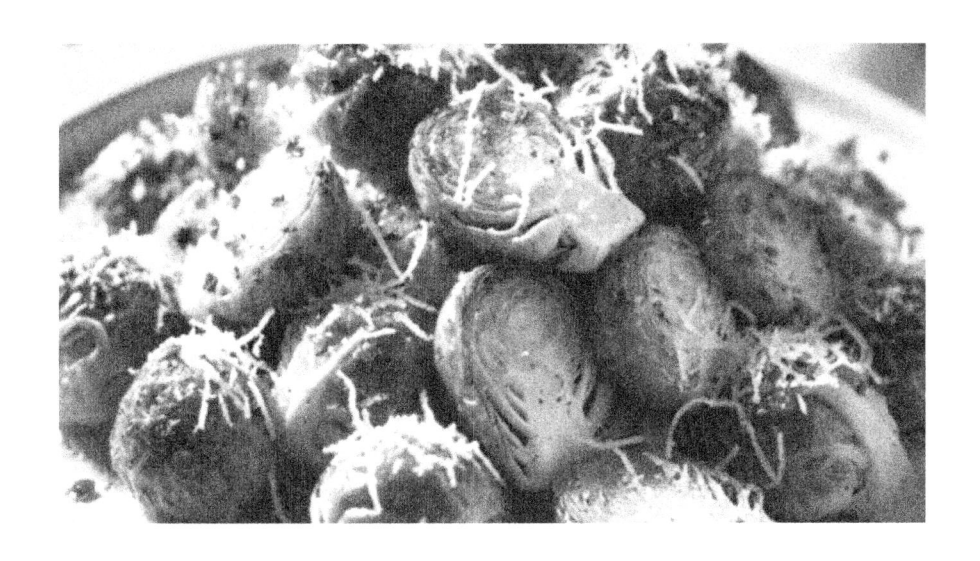

PARMESAN ROASTED BRUSSELS SPROUTS

Ingredients

- 2 cups Brussels sprouts, halved (76 calories)
- ¼ cup grated Parmesan cheese (110 calories)
- 1 tablespoon olive oil (120 calories)
- Salt and pepper to taste (0 calories)
- Fresh herbs for garnish (optional, 0 calories)

Total Calories: Approximately 306 calories (serves 2, about 153 calories per serving)

Instructions

1. Preheat your oven to 400°F (200°C).
2. Toss the halved Brussels sprouts in olive oil, salt, and pepper.
3. Spread the Brussels sprouts on a baking sheet in a single layer.
4. Roast for 20-25 minutes, turning halfway through, until the sprouts are golden brown and crispy on the edges.
5. Remove from the oven and sprinkle the grated Parmesan cheese over the top.
6. Return to the oven for an additional 5 minutes, until the cheese is melted and slightly crispy.
7. Garnish with fresh herbs if desired and serve hot.

Tips And Tricks

- For an extra flavor kick, add a splash of balsamic vinegar before roasting.
- If you like your Brussels sprouts extra crispy, broil them for the last 1-2 minutes of roasting.

Tools Required

- Baking sheet
- Mixing bowl

Fun Fact

Brussels sprouts are part of the cruciferous vegetable family, which includes broccoli and cauliflower, and they're packed with vitamins, fiber, and antioxidants.

Possible Ingredient Substitutions

- Use nutritional yeast instead of Parmesan for a dairy-free alternative.
- Swap olive oil with avocado oil for a different flavor profile.

LIGHT CHEESY MASHED POTATOES

Ingredients

- 2 medium potatoes, peeled and diced (330 calories)
- ½ cup shredded low-fat cheddar cheese (160 calories)
- ¼ cup skim milk (22 calories)
- 1 tablespoon light cream cheese (30 calories)
- Salt and pepper to taste (0 calories)
- Fresh herbs for garnish (optional, 0 calories)

Total Calories: Approximately 542 calories (serves 4, about 136 calories per serving)

Instructions

1. Boil the diced potatoes in salted water for 10-12 minutes, or until tender.
2. Drain the potatoes and return them to the pot.
3. Add the shredded cheddar cheese, cream cheese, and skim milk to the potatoes. Mash until smooth and creamy.
4. Season with salt and pepper to taste.
5. Serve the mashed potatoes hot, garnished with fresh herbs and an extra sprinkle of cheese if desired.

Tips And Tricks

- For extra creaminess, you can add a bit more milk or cream cheese.
- Try adding roasted garlic for a flavorful twist on this classic side dish.

Tools Required

- Potato masher
- Large pot for boiling

Fun Fact

Mashed potatoes are a classic comfort food, but using light cheese and cream keeps this version lower in calories without sacrificing flavor!

Possible Ingredient Substitutions

- Use sweet potatoes instead of regular potatoes for a more nutrient-dense option.

- Swap cheddar for Parmesan or mozzarella for a different cheesy flavor.

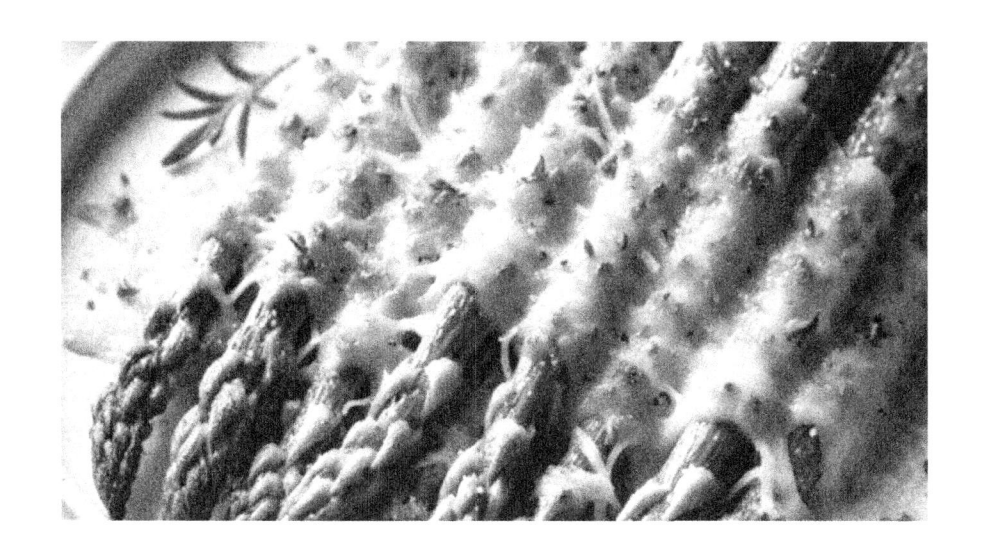

CHEESY BAKED ASPARAGUS

Ingredients

- 1 bunch asparagus, trimmed (90 calories)
- ¼ cup shredded low-fat mozzarella cheese (80 calories)
- 2 tablespoons grated Parmesan cheese (44 calories)
- 1 tablespoon olive oil (120 calories)
- Salt and pepper to taste (0 calories)
- Fresh herbs for garnish (optional, 0 calories)

Total Calories: Approximately 334 calories (serves 2, about 167 calories per serving)

Instructions

1. Preheat the oven to 400°F (200°C).
2. Place the asparagus on a baking sheet and drizzle with olive oil. Season with salt and pepper.
3. Bake for 10-12 minutes, or until the asparagus is tender.
4. Remove from the oven and sprinkle the shredded mozzarella and grated Parmesan over the top.
5. Return to the oven and bake for another 5 minutes, or until the cheese is melted and bubbly.
6. Garnish with fresh herbs if desired and serve hot.

Tips And Tricks

- For extra flavor, you can add a squeeze of lemon juice over the asparagus before serving.
- To make the dish even crispier, broil the asparagus for the last 1-2 minutes of baking.

Tools Required

- Baking sheet
- Tongs for tossing the asparagus

Fun Fact

Asparagus is packed with vitamins A, C, and K, making it a nutritious vegetable that pairs well with the rich flavor of cheese!

Possible Ingredient Substitutions

- Use cheddar cheese instead of mozzarella for a sharper flavor.
- Try adding a sprinkle of garlic powder or red pepper flakes for extra spice.

GRILLED CORN WITH CHEESE TOPPING

Ingredients

- 2 ears of corn (180 calories)
- ¼ cup shredded low-fat cheddar cheese (80 calories)
- 2 tablespoons grated Parmesan cheese (44 calories)
- 1 tablespoon olive oil (120 calories)
- Fresh herbs for garnish (optional, 0 calories)
- Salt and pepper to taste (0 calories)

Total Calories: Approximately 424 calories (serves 2, about 212 calories per serving)

Instructions

1. Preheat your grill to medium-high heat.
2. Brush the ears of corn with olive oil and season with salt and pepper.
3. Grill the corn for about 10-12 minutes, turning occasionally, until the kernels are charred and tender.
4. Remove the corn from the grill and sprinkle with the shredded cheddar cheese and grated Parmesan while it's still hot.
5. Garnish with fresh herbs if desired and serve immediately.

Tips And Tricks

- You can add a squeeze of lime juice for a fresh citrus twist.
- For a smoky flavor, sprinkle a pinch of smoked paprika on top of the cheese.

Tools Required

- Grill or grill pan
- Tongs for turning the corn

Fun Fact

Corn is a summer favorite and grilling it brings out its natural sweetness. Pairing it with cheese adds a savory richness that's hard to resist!

Possible Ingredient Substitutions

- Use feta cheese instead of cheddar for a Mediterranean

twist.

- Swap olive oil for butter if you prefer a richer flavor.

RICOTTA CHEESE & HONEY DESSERT

Ingredients

- ½ cup ricotta cheese (120 calories)
- 1 tablespoon honey (64 calories)
- A few fresh berries (optional, 10 calories)
- Fresh mint leaves for garnish (optional, 0 calories)

Total Calories: Approximately 194 calories

Instructions

1. In a small bowl, spoon the ricotta cheese and smooth it out with the back of a spoon.
2. Drizzle the honey evenly over the ricotta.

3. Garnish with a few fresh berries and mint leaves for a pop of color and flavor.
4. Serve immediately as a light and refreshing dessert.

Tips And Tricks

- For added crunch, sprinkle some crushed almonds or pistachios on top.
- You can use flavored honey, like lavender or cinnamon, to enhance the taste.

Tools Required

- Small bowl
- Spoon for drizzling

Fun Fact

Ricotta cheese is lower in fat than many other cheeses, making it a great option for a lighter dessert that still feels indulgent.

Possible Ingredient Substitutions

- Use Greek yogurt instead of ricotta for a different creamy base.
- Replace honey with agave syrup for a vegan-friendly option.

LOW CALORIE CHEESECAKE BITES

Ingredients

- 1 cup low-fat cream cheese (160 calories)
- ¼ cup Greek yogurt (30 calories)
- 2 tablespoons honey or maple syrup (128 calories)
- 1 teaspoon vanilla extract (5 calories)
- ½ cup crushed graham crackers (180 calories)
- Fresh berries for topping (optional, 10 calories)

Total Calories: Approximately 513 calories (makes 12 bites, about 43 calories per bite)

Instructions

1. In a bowl, mix the low-fat cream cheese, Greek yogurt, honey (or maple syrup), and vanilla extract until smooth and creamy.
2. Line a mini muffin tin with liners and press about 1 teaspoon of crushed graham crackers into the bottom of each cup to form the crust.
3. Spoon the cheesecake mixture evenly into each cup on top of the graham cracker base.
4. Refrigerate for at least 2 hours, or until the cheesecake bites are firm.
5. Top with fresh berries and serve chilled.

Tips And Tricks

- You can freeze these cheesecake bites for a longer-lasting treat.
- Add a drizzle of berry sauce or dark chocolate for extra indulgence.

Tools Required

- Mini muffin tin
- Mixing bowl
- Spoon for pressing the crust

Fun Fact

Cheesecake can be made lighter by using Greek yogurt and low-fat cream cheese, giving you all the creaminess without the guilt!

Possible Ingredient Substitutions

- Use a gluten-free graham cracker base if needed.
- Swap honey for a low-calorie sweetener to reduce the calorie count further.

COTTAGE CHEESE & CINNAMON DELIGHT

Ingredients

- ½ cup low-fat cottage cheese (90 calories)
- 1 teaspoon honey (20 calories)
- ½ teaspoon ground cinnamon (3 calories)
- ½ apple, sliced (45 calories)
- 1 tablespoon chopped walnuts (optional, 45 calories)

Total Calories: Approximately 158 calories

Instructions

1. In a small bowl, add the cottage cheese as the base.

2. Drizzle the honey over the cottage cheese and sprinkle with ground cinnamon.
3. Garnish with fresh apple slices and, if desired, a sprinkle of chopped walnuts for extra crunch.
4. Serve immediately as a cozy, protein-packed snack or dessert.

Tips And Tricks

- You can use different fruits like pears or bananas depending on your preference.
- For a sweeter treat, increase the amount of honey or add a pinch of vanilla extract.

Tools Required

- Small bowl
- Spoon for drizzling

Fun Fact

Cinnamon is known for its anti-inflammatory properties, and pairing it with protein-rich cottage cheese makes this snack both nutritious and satisfying!

Possible Ingredient Substitutions

- Use agave syrup or maple syrup instead of honey for a diffcrent flavor profile.
- Add a handful of granola on top for added texture and crunch.

CHEESE-STUFFED DATES

Ingredients

- 8 large Medjool dates, pitted (200 calories)
- ¼ cup low-fat cream cheese (80 calories)
- 1 tablespoon crumbled blue cheese or feta (25 calories)
- 2 tablespoons chopped walnuts or almonds (90 calories)
- Fresh herbs for garnish (optional, 0 calories)

Total Calories: Approximately 395 calories (makes 8 stuffed dates, about 50 calories per date)

Instructions

1. Slice the dates lengthwise and remove the pits.

2. In a small bowl, mix the cream cheese and blue cheese (or feta) until smooth.
3. Stuff each date with a spoonful of the cheese mixture.
4. Top the stuffed dates with chopped walnuts or almonds for added crunch.
5. Garnish with fresh herbs if desired and serve as an appetizer or a sweet snack.

Tips And Tricks

- You can experiment with different cheeses like goat cheese or ricotta for different flavor profiles.
- For a sweeter touch, drizzle the dates with honey or maple syrup.

Tools Required

- Small bowl for mixing
- Knife for slicing the dates

Fun Fact

Dates are naturally sweet and rich in fiber, making them a great base for savory fillings like cheese, creating a perfect balance of flavors!

Possible Ingredient Substitutions

- Use vegan cream cheese for a dairy-free version.
- Substitute the walnuts with pistachios for a more vibrant and crunchy topping.

GREEK YOGURT & CREAM CHEESE FROSTING WITH BERRIES

Ingredients

- ¼ cup Greek yogurt (30 calories)
- ¼ cup low-fat cream cheese (80 calories)
- 1 tablespoon honey or maple syrup (64 calories)
- ½ teaspoon vanilla extract (5 calories)
- ½ cup mixed berries (strawberries, blueberries, raspberries) (35 calories)
- Fresh mint leaves for garnish (optional, 0 calories)

Total Calories: Approximately 214 calories

Instructions

1. In a small bowl, mix the Greek yogurt, low-fat cream cheese, honey (or maple syrup), and vanilla extract until smooth and creamy.
2. Spoon the frosting into a serving dish.
3. Top with mixed berries and garnish with fresh mint leaves.
4. Serve immediately as a light and refreshing dessert.

Tips And Tricks

- You can use this frosting as a topping for cakes, muffins, or pancakes.
- Adjust the sweetness to your taste by adding more or less honey or syrup.

Tools Required

- Mixing bowl
- Spoon for stirring

Fun Fact

Greek yogurt is high in protein and adds a tangy creaminess to this light frosting, making it a healthier alternative to traditional buttercream.

Possible Ingredient Substitutions

- Use agave syrup or a low-calorie sweetener for a lower

sugar version.

- Swap out the berries for other fruits like sliced peaches or kiwis.

CHEESE-STUFFED MINI BELL PEPPERS

Ingredients

- 12 mini bell peppers, halved and seeded (96 calories)
- ½ cup low-fat cream cheese (80 calories)
- ½ cup shredded low-fat cheddar cheese (160 calories)
- 1 tablespoon fresh herbs (like chives or parsley) (0 calories)
- Salt and pepper to taste (0 calories)
- 1 tablespoon breadcrumbs (optional, 20 calories)

Total Calories: Approximately 356 calories (makes 12 stuffed peppers, about 30 calories per pepper)

Instructions

1. Preheat your oven to 375°F (190°C).
2. In a bowl, mix together the cream cheese, shredded cheddar cheese, chopped herbs, salt, and pepper until smooth.
3. Stuff each halved mini bell pepper with the cheese mixture, pressing down gently to pack it in.
4. If desired, sprinkle breadcrumbs on top of each stuffed pepper for added crunch.
5. Arrange the stuffed peppers on a baking sheet and bake for 15-20 minutes, or until the cheese is melted and the peppers are tender.
6. Serve hot as an appetizer or snack.

Tips And Tricks

- For extra flavor, you can add spices like garlic powder or smoked paprika to the cheese mixture.
- These can be made ahead of time and baked just before serving.

Tools Required

- Baking sheet
- Mixing bowl

Fun Fact

Mini bell peppers are not only sweet and colorful but also packed with vitamins A and C, making this dish a nutritious choice!

Possible Ingredient Substitutions

- Use goat cheese instead of cream cheese for a tangy flavor.
- Substitute the cheddar with a different cheese like feta or mozzarella for variety.

LOW-CALORIE CHEESE NACHOS

Ingredients

- 2 cups baked whole grain tortilla chips (200 calories)
- ½ cup shredded low-fat cheddar cheese (160 calories)
- ½ cup diced tomatoes (15 calories)
- 1 jalapeño, sliced (5 calories)
- 2 tablespoons fresh cilantro or parsley for garnish (optional, 1 calorie)
- Salsa for serving (optional, 10 calories)

Total Calories: Approximately 371 calories (serves 2, about 186 calories per serving)

Instructions

1. Preheat your oven to 350°F (175°C).
2. Spread the baked tortilla chips evenly on a baking sheet.
3. Sprinkle the shredded cheddar cheese over the chips.
4. Top with diced tomatoes and jalapeño slices.
5. Bake for 5-7 minutes, or until the cheese is melted and bubbly.
6. Remove from the oven and garnish with fresh cilantro or parsley if desired.
7. Serve hot with salsa on the side.

Tips And Tricks

- Feel free to add other toppings like black beans, corn, or avocado for more flavor and nutrition.
- For extra spice, use pepper jack cheese instead of cheddar.

Tools Required

- Baking sheet
- Spoon for topping

Fun Fact

Nachos originated in Mexico and have evolved into countless variations, making them a versatile snack for any occasion!

Possible Ingredient Substitutions

- Use low-carb tortilla chips for a lower-carb version.
- Swap cheddar cheese for a dairy-free cheese alternative.

CHEESY ZUCCHINI FRITTERS

Ingredients

- 2 medium zucchinis, grated (60 calories)
- ½ cup shredded low-fat cheddar cheese (160 calories)
- 1 large egg (70 calories)
- ¼ cup whole wheat flour (90 calories)
- 1 clove garlic, minced (4 calories)
- Salt and pepper to taste (0 calories)
- 1 tablespoon olive oil for frying (120 calories)
- Fresh herbs for garnish (optional, 0 calories)

Total Calories: Approximately 504 calories (makes about 6 fritters, about 84 calories per fritter)

Instructions

1. Place the grated zucchini in a clean kitchen towel and squeeze out the excess moisture.
2. In a mixing bowl, combine the grated zucchini, shredded cheese, egg, flour, garlic, salt, and pepper. Mix until well combined.
3. Heat the olive oil in a skillet over medium heat.
4. Spoon the zucchini mixture into the skillet, forming small fritters. Flatten them slightly with a spatula.
5. Cook for 3-4 minutes on each side, or until golden brown and crispy.
6. Remove from the skillet and place on a paper towel to absorb excess oil.
7. Garnish with fresh herbs if desired and serve warm with yogurt or sour cream.

Tips And Tricks

- You can add grated carrots or corn for extra flavor and nutrition.
- Serve with a squeeze of lemon for a refreshing twist.

Tools Required

- Mixing bowl
- Skillet
- Spatula

Fun Fact

Zucchini fritters are a great way to incorporate vegetables into your diet while enjoying a tasty snack!

Possible Ingredient Substitutions

- Use gluten-free flour if you prefer a gluten-free version.
- Swap cheddar for feta or goat cheese for a different flavor profile.

CHEESE AND VEGGIE QUICHE CUPS

Ingredients

- 4 large eggs (280 calories)
- ½ cup shredded low-fat cheddar cheese (80 calories)
- 1 cup fresh spinach, chopped (7 calories)
- ½ cup bell peppers, diced (12 calories)
- ¼ cup diced onions (12 calories)
- 1 tablespoon olive oil (120 calories)
- Salt and pepper to taste (0 calories)
- 6 mini phyllo pastry cups or muffin cups (optional, 150 calories)

Total Calories: Approximately 669 calories (makes 6 quiche cups, about 112 calories per cup without pastry cups)

Instructions

1. Preheat your oven to 375°F (190°C).
2. Heat olive oil in a skillet over medium heat. Sauté the onions and bell peppers until softened, about 3-4 minutes. Add the chopped spinach and cook until wilted. Remove from heat.
3. In a bowl, whisk the eggs, then stir in the sautéed vegetables and shredded cheese. Season with salt and pepper.
4. If using mini pastry cups, place them on a baking sheet. If not, grease a muffin tin.
5. Pour the egg and veggie mixture into each pastry cup or muffin cup, filling about ¾ full.
6. Bake for 15-20 minutes, or until the egg is set and the tops are golden.
7. Allow to cool slightly before removing from the muffin tin or serving.

Tips And Tricks

- Feel free to add other vegetables like mushrooms or zucchini for extra flavor.
- These quiche cups can be made ahead of time and stored in the refrigerator for a quick breakfast or snack.

Tools Required

- Skillet
- Muffin tin or baking sheet

- Mixing bowl

Fun Fact

Quiche is a versatile dish that can be enjoyed for breakfast, lunch, or dinner, and can easily be customized with various fillings!

Possible Ingredient Substitutions

- Use egg whites instead of whole eggs for a lower-calorie option.
- Substitute the cheddar with feta or goat cheese for a different flavor.

COTTAGE CHEESE & CUCUMBER SALAD

Ingredients

- 1 cup low-fat cottage cheese (90 calories)
- 1 medium cucumber, diced (16 calories)
- ¼ cup diced red onion (12 calories)
- 1 tablespoon fresh dill or parsley (optional, 0 calories)
- Salt and pepper to taste (0 calories)

Total Calories: Approximately 118 calories

Instructions

1. In a mixing bowl, combine the cottage cheese, diced

cucumber, and red onion.
2. Stir in the fresh herbs (if using) and season with salt and pepper to taste.
3. Serve immediately as a light salad or refrigerate for 30 minutes to let the flavors meld.

Tips And Tricks

- For added flavor, you can include a squeeze of lemon juice or a dash of vinegar.
- This salad pairs well with grilled meats or as a refreshing side dish for picnics.

Tools Required

- Mixing bowl
- Knife for dicing

Fun Fact

Cottage cheese is a great source of protein, and when combined with refreshing cucumbers, it makes for a nutritious and satisfying salad!

Possible Ingredient Substitutions

- Use Greek yogurt instead of cottage cheese for a creamier texture.
- Add cherry tomatoes or bell peppers for more color and flavor.

CHEESY BAKED TOMATOES

Ingredients

- 4 medium tomatoes, halved (60 calories)
- ½ cup shredded low-fat mozzarella cheese (160 calories)
- ¼ cup grated Parmesan cheese (110 calories)
- 1 tablespoon olive oil (120 calories)
- Salt and pepper to taste (0 calories)
- Fresh basil leaves for garnish (optional, 0 calories)

Total Calories: Approximately 450 calories (serves 4, about 113 calories per serving)

Instructions

1. Preheat your oven to 375°F (190°C).
2. Place the halved tomatoes on a baking sheet and drizzle with olive oil. Season with salt and pepper.
3. Sprinkle shredded mozzarella and grated Parmesan cheese on top of each tomato half.
4. Bake for 15-20 minutes, or until the cheese is melted and golden brown.
5. Remove from the oven and garnish with fresh basil leaves before serving.

Tips And Tricks

- For extra flavor, add a sprinkle of garlic powder or Italian herbs on top before baking.
- These can be served as a side dish or as a light appetizer.

Tools Required

- Baking sheet
- Knife for slicing tomatoes

Fun Fact

Baked tomatoes are not only delicious but also packed with antioxidants like lycopene, which may help reduce the risk of certain diseases.

Possible Ingredient Substitutions

- Use any cheese you prefer, like cheddar or goat cheese, for different flavors.
- Substitute the olive oil with a non-stick spray for a lighter version.

CHEESE AND APPLE SLICES

Ingredients

- 1 medium apple, sliced (95 calories)
- 2 ounces of cheese (such as cheddar or gouda) (140 calories)
- Fresh mint leaves for garnish (optional, 0 calories)

Total Calories: Approximately 235 calories

Instructions

1. Slice the apple into thin wedges or rounds.
2. Cut the cheese into cubes or slices.
3. Arrange the apple slices and cheese on a plate.

4. Garnish with fresh mint leaves if desired.
5. Serve immediately as a light snack or appetizer.

Tips And Tricks

- For added flavor, drizzle a little honey over the apples before serving.
- This combination is great for a quick snack, offering a nice balance of sweet and savory flavors.

Tools Required

- Knife for slicing
- Serving plate

Fun Fact

The combination of cheese and apples is not only delicious but also provides a good mix of protein, fat, and carbohydrates, making it a satisfying snack!

Possible Ingredient Substitutions

- Use any cheese of your choice, such as brie or goat cheese, for different flavor profiles.
- Try other fruits like pears or grapes for variety.

CHEESY SPINACH DIP

Ingredients

- 1 cup chopped fresh spinach (7 calories)
- ½ cup low-fat cream cheese (80 calories)
- ½ cup shredded low-fat mozzarella cheese (160 calories)
- ¼ cup Greek yogurt (30 calories)
- 1 clove garlic, minced (4 calories)
- Salt and pepper to taste (0 calories)
- Tortilla chips or fresh veggies for serving (optional, calorie count varies)

Total Calories: Approximately 281 calories (without chips or veggies)

Instructions

1. In a skillet, heat over medium heat and sauté the minced garlic for 1-2 minutes until fragrant.
2. Add the chopped spinach to the skillet and cook until wilted.
3. In a mixing bowl, combine the cream cheese, Greek yogurt, and shredded mozzarella. Mix until smooth.
4. Stir the sautéed spinach and garlic into the cheese mixture. Season with salt and pepper.
5. Transfer the mixture to a baking dish and bake at 375°F (190°C) for 15-20 minutes, or until the cheese is melted and bubbly.
6. Serve warm with tortilla chips or fresh vegetables for dipping.

Tips And Tricks

- For a spicy kick, add a dash of red pepper flakes or chopped jalapeños to the mix.
- You can make this dip ahead of time and bake it just before serving.

Tools Required

- Skillet
- Mixing bowl
- Baking dish

Fun Fact

Spinach is not only delicious but also packed with vitamins and minerals, making this cheesy dip a healthier choice for gatherings!

Possible Ingredient Substitutions

- Use cottage cheese instead of cream cheese for a lighter version.
- Swap mozzarella for cheddar or a cheese blend for a different flavor.

CHEESE-STUFFED CHICKEN BREAST

Ingredients

- 2 boneless, skinless chicken breasts (300 calories)
- ½ cup low-fat cream cheese (80 calories)
- ¼ cup shredded mozzarella cheese (80 calories)
- 1 tablespoon fresh herbs (such as basil or parsley) (0 calories)
- Salt and pepper to taste (0 calories)
- 1 tablespoon olive oil (120 calories)

Total Calories: Approximately 580 calories (for 2 servings, about 290 calories per serving)

Instructions

1. Preheat your oven to 375°F (190°C).
2. In a mixing bowl, combine the cream cheese, mozzarella, and fresh herbs. Season with salt and pepper.
3. Slice a pocket into each chicken breast, being careful not to cut all the way through.
4. Stuff each chicken breast with the cheese mixture, securing with toothpicks if necessary.
5. Heat olive oil in an oven-safe skillet over medium heat. Sear the stuffed chicken breasts for 3-4 minutes on each side until golden brown.
6. Transfer the skillet to the preheated oven and bake for 20-25 minutes, or until the chicken is cooked through and the cheese is melted.
7. Let it rest for a few minutes before slicing. Serve hot, garnished with additional fresh herbs if desired.

Tips And Tricks

- Serve with a side of roasted vegetables or a fresh salad for a complete meal.
- You can add garlic or onion powder to the cheese mixture for extra flavor.

Tools Required

- Mixing bowl
- Skillet (oven-safe)

- Toothpicks (if needed)

Fun Fact

Stuffed chicken breasts are a delicious way to keep the meat juicy while adding flavor with cheesy fillings!

Possible Ingredient Substitutions

- Use ricotta cheese instead of cream cheese for a different texture.
- Substitute the mozzarella for any cheese of your choice, like feta or goat cheese.

GRILLED CHEESE ROLL-UPS

Ingredients

- 4 slices of whole grain bread (240 calories)
- 1 cup shredded low-fat cheddar cheese (160 calories)
- 1 tablespoon butter or olive oil for toasting (100 calories)

Total Calories: Approximately 500 calories (makes 4 roll-ups, about 125 calories per roll-up)

Instructions

1. Preheat a skillet over medium heat.
2. Flatten each slice of bread with a rolling pin to make it

easier to roll up.

3. Place a generous amount of shredded cheese on one end of each slice of bread.
4. Roll the bread tightly around the cheese.
5. Spread butter or olive oil on the outside of each roll-up.
6. Place the roll-ups seam-side down in the skillet and toast for 2-3 minutes on each side, or until golden brown and the cheese is melted.
7. Cut into bite-sized pieces and serve hot.

Tips And Tricks

- For added flavor, you can sprinkle garlic powder or herbs inside the roll-ups before rolling.
- These are great served with marinara sauce or a side salad.

Tools Required

- Skillet
- Rolling pin

Fun Fact

Grilled cheese roll-ups are a fun twist on the classic grilled cheese sandwich, perfect for kids and adults alike!

Possible Ingredient Substitutions

- Use gluten-free bread if needed.
- Substitute cheddar cheese for mozzarella or a cheese

blend for different flavors.

BROCCOLI AND CHEESE BITES

Ingredients

- 2 cups finely chopped broccoli (62 calories)
- ½ cup shredded low-fat cheddar cheese (160 calories)
- ¼ cup breadcrumbs (110 calories)
- 1 large egg (70 calories)
- 1 clove garlic, minced (4 calories)
- Salt and pepper to taste (0 calories)
- 1 tablespoon olive oil (120 calories)

Total Calories: Approximately 526 calories (makes about 12 bites, about 44 calories per bite)

Instructions

1. Preheat your oven to 375°F (190°C) and line a baking sheet with parchment paper.
2. In a mixing bowl, combine the finely chopped broccoli, shredded cheese, breadcrumbs, egg, minced garlic, salt, and pepper. Mix well until combined.
3. Form the mixture into small balls and place them on the prepared baking sheet.
4. Drizzle the tops with olive oil.
5. Bake for 15-20 minutes, or until the bites are golden brown and crispy.
6. Allow to cool slightly before serving.

Tips And Tricks

- For extra flavor, add a pinch of red pepper flakes or Italian seasoning to the mixture.
- These bites can be served with a dipping sauce like ranch or marinara.

Tools Required

- Mixing bowl
- Baking sheet

Fun Fact

Broccoli and cheese bites are a delicious way to get your greens while enjoying the comfort of cheesy snacks!

Possible Ingredient Substitutions

- Use gluten-free breadcrumbs if desired.
- Swap cheddar cheese for mozzarella or any cheese of your choice.

CHEESE AND AVOCADO TOAST

Ingredients

- 1 slice whole grain bread (70 calories)
- ½ ripe avocado, mashed (120 calories)
- 1 ounce sliced cheese (such as feta or cheddar) (100 calories)
- Salt and pepper to taste (0 calories)
- Fresh herbs for garnish (optional, 0 calories)

Total Calories: Approximately 290 calories

Instructions

1. Toast the whole grain bread until golden brown.
2. In a small bowl, mash the avocado and season with salt and pepper.
3. Spread the mashed avocado evenly over the toasted bread.
4. Top with slices of cheese.
5. Garnish with fresh herbs if desired.
6. Serve immediately as a nutritious breakfast or snack.

Tips And Tricks

- For added flavor, drizzle a little lemon juice over the avocado before adding the cheese.
- You can also add toppings like sliced tomatoes, radishes, or a poached egg for extra nutrition.

Tools Required

- Toaster
- Knife for spreading

Fun Fact

Avocado is packed with healthy fats and nutrients, making it a great complement to the protein-rich cheese on your toast!

Possible Ingredient Substitutions

- Use gluten-free bread if needed.
- Swap cheese for a plant-based option to make it dairy-free.

NUTRITIONAL HIGHLIGHTS

Incorporating cheese and vegetables into your diet can provide a wealth of health benefits.

Cheese:

- **Protein Source:** Cheese is an excellent source of protein, which is essential for building and repairing tissues, as well as maintaining muscle mass.
- **Calcium-Rich:** Many types of cheese are rich in calcium, crucial for maintaining strong bones and teeth, and supporting overall bone health.
- **Vitamins and Minerals:** Cheese contains important vitamins such as B12, which is essential for nerve function and the production of red blood cells, and A, which supports vision and immune function.

Vegetables:

- **Nutrient-Dense:** Vegetables are low in calories but high in essential vitamins and minerals, making them a great choice for a healthy diet.
- **Fiber-Rich:** Many vegetables are high in dietary fiber, which aids in digestion, helps maintain a healthy weight, and lowers the risk of chronic diseases.

- **Antioxidants:** Vegetables provide a variety of antioxidants that help protect your body from oxidative stress and reduce inflammation.

Combining cheese and vegetables in your meals not only enhances flavor but also creates a balanced dish that supports overall health. Enjoy these recipes as a delicious way to nourish your body!

COOKING TIPS

1. **Selecting Fresh Ingredients:**
   - Choose fresh, in-season vegetables for the best flavor and nutritional value. Look for vibrant colors and firm textures when selecting produce.

2. **Prepping Vegetables:**
   - Wash and dry your vegetables thoroughly before cooking to remove any dirt or pesticides. For leafy greens, consider using a salad spinner to remove excess water.

3. **Maximizing Flavor:**
   - Enhance the natural flavors of your ingredients by using herbs and spices. Fresh herbs like basil, parsley, or cilantro can elevate a dish, while spices like garlic powder, paprika, or black pepper add depth.

4. **Cheese Melting Tips:**
   - For a smooth melt, let cheese come to room temperature before cooking. Shredding cheese rather than using whole slices can also help it melt more evenly.

5. **Balancing Textures:**
   - Incorporate a variety of textures in your dishes by combining creamy cheeses with crunchy vegetables. This not only makes meals more enjoyable but also more visually appealing.

6. **Experimenting with Pairings:**
    - Don't be afraid to mix different cheeses with various vegetables. Each combination can create a unique flavor profile, so feel free to get creative!

By following these simple tips, you can enhance the flavors of your dishes and create meals that are both delicious and satisfying!

SERVING SUGGESTIONS

1. **Pairing with Fresh Salads:**
    - Serve your cheese and vegetable dishes alongside a light, fresh salad. A simple mixed greens salad with a vinaigrette dressing complements the richness of cheesy recipes nicely.

2. **Accompanying Whole Grains:**
    - Consider pairing dishes with whole grains like quinoa, brown rice, or whole grain bread. These add texture and provide additional fiber, making for a balanced meal.

3. **Adding a Protein Source:**
    - For a complete meal, serve cheese and vegetable dishes with a source of lean protein such as grilled chicken, fish, or legumes. This adds satiety and balances the flavors.

4. **Complementing with Dips:**
    - Pair cheesy appetizers with dips like hummus, salsa, or tzatziki. These add an extra layer of flavor and can make for a fun, shareable snack.

5. **Choosing the Right Beverage:**
    - Consider serving with beverages that enhance the flavors of the dishes. Light white wines, sparkling water with lemon, or herbal teas can complement cheesy flavors well.

6. **Offering a Cheese Board:**

- Create a simple cheese board featuring a variety of cheeses, fresh fruits, and crunchy nuts. This is great for gatherings and allows guests to mix and match flavors.

These serving suggestions can help you create a well-rounded meal experience that is both delicious and visually appealing!

CONCLUSION

Thank you for exploring these delightful cheese and vegetable recipes! We hope you find joy in preparing and savoring these dishes, whether for yourself, family, or friends.

Cooking is not just about nourishing the body; it's also about creating connections and making memories around the table. We encourage you to share these recipes with loved ones, inspire creativity in the kitchen, and experiment with your own variations.

Embrace the flavors, enjoy the process, and most importantly, have fun! Every meal is an opportunity to bring people together and celebrate the joy of good food. Happy cooking!

WE APPRECIATE YOUR FEEDBACK!

Thank you for exploring the recipes in this cookbook! If you enjoyed the dishes, we invite you to share your thoughts in a review. Your feedback helps others discover these delicious recipes.

Thank you for your support, and happy cooking!